Table Manners
for
YOUNG BARBARIANS

I0167526

**Robert Wayne Bode and
Elizabeth Bode**

Published in 2022 by
Saratoga Springs Publishing, LLC
Saratoga Springs, NY 12866
www.SaratogaSpringsPublishing.com
Printed in the United States of America

ISBN-13: 978-1-955568-09-8
ISBN-10: 1-955568-09-X
Library of Congress Control Number: 2022911004
Text and illustrations Copyright © 2022
Robert Wayne Bode and Elizabeth Bode

Written by Robert Wayne Bode and Elizabeth Bode
Illustrations by Robert Wayne Bode
Graphic Design by Emily Brooks
Publisher & Book design by Vicki Addesso Dodd

This book is a work of fiction. Any references to historical events, real
people or real locales are used fictitiously. Other names, characters, places
and incidents are the product of the author's imagination and any resemblance
to actual events or locales or persons, living or dead, is entirely coincidental.

All rights reserved. No portion of this book may be reproduced
or transmitted in any form or by any means, electronic, mechanical,
photocopying, recording, or by any information storage or
retrieval system without written permission from the
publisher and copyright holder.

Saratoga Springs Publishing's books are
available at a discount when purchased in quantity for
promotions, fundraising and educational use. For additional
information, book sales or events, contact us at
www.RobertBode.com or
BobandBethBode@gmail.com

Special thanks to Amy Bode,
Bruce Bode, and Flossie Bode for their
helpful suggestions, to Doris Libolt for
suggesting the concept of "Barbarians,"
and to Vicki Addesso Dodd
for once again making a book idea
become a reality.

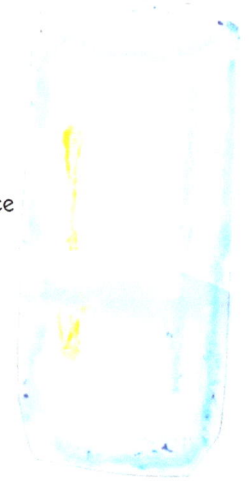

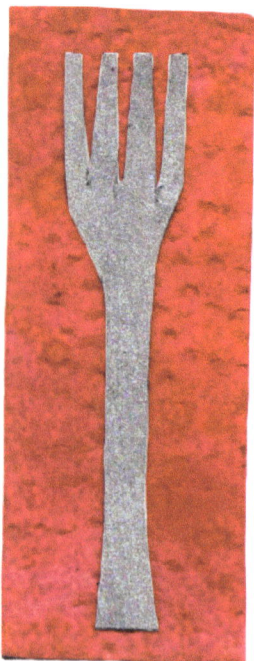

Caleb and Lila sat at the table,
Big slurps and burps filled the air,
Eating as fast as they were able,
A most unmannered pair.

Grandma meanwhile looked on, distraught,
Her eyebrows raised in dismay.
"This will never do," she thought,
"We must make a change today."

"Dear Caleb and Lila," she sweetly said,
"Let's have a little chat,
It's your eating habits, I'm afraid,
We have to talk about that."

"I'd like to tell you all the things
My grandma said to us,
Not fancy dining like with kings,
Just nice and courteous."

Some call them rules of etiquette,
Some say table manners.
But of one thing I'm definite,
Good behavior matters.

The first rule is, before each meal,
You've got to wash your hands.
That dirt is dirty, those germs are real!
Make sure you understand.

Think of what those hands have touched,
Some pretty dreadful places,
But all those grimy germs and such,
Soap and water erases.

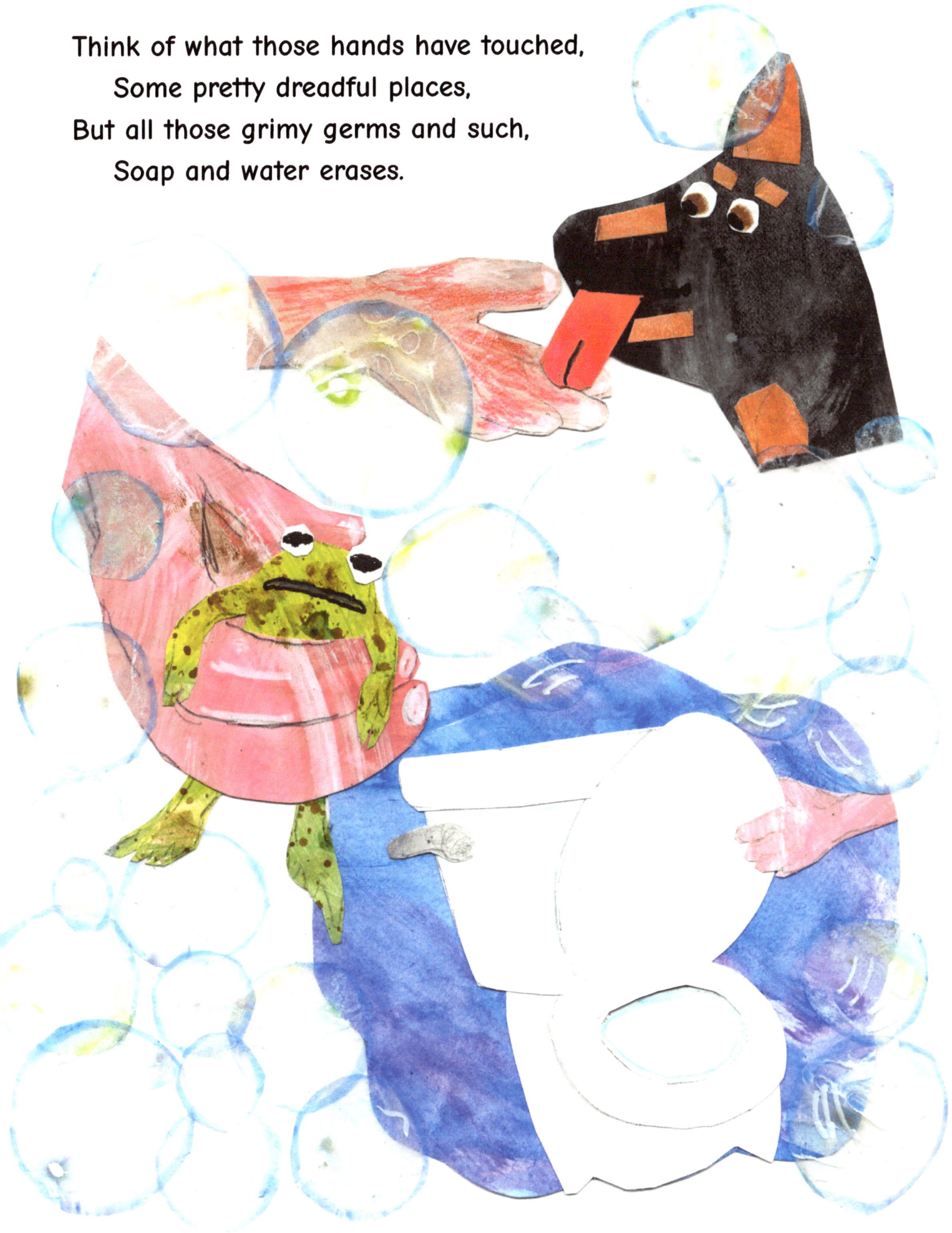

Let's say you're at the table seated,
Your hands all shiny and clean,
There's one more thing to be completed
Before that tasty cuisine.

Take off your hat and stay a while,
And with head slightly bowed,
You might ask a blessing on the meal,
Silently or right out loud.

Now you might notice in front of you
A napkin of paper or cloth,
It's there for when some wiping is due
For your fingers or your mouth.

For now it needs to be put some place,
Your lap's the place for that napkin.
So put it there neatly just in case,
Until it's called to action.

Resting your elbows on the table
Is usually considered taboo.
Try to remember if you are able,
It's not the right thing to do.

Some of these rules are not so strict,
The elbows rule, we mean.
For daily meals it might be skipped,
But not when with the Queen!

Reaching in front of someone, we're taught,
Is most sure to cause a stir.
If everyone grabbed the grub they sought,
A frightful scene might occur.

From a serving dish in front of you,
Just take a modest portion.
Then pass it to the left of you,
Be courteous to that person.

To the left of your plate lies the fork,
Used for scooping or stabbing,
For greens, or beans, or carrots, or pork,
And all foods suited for jabbing.

Then there's the spoon for you to seize,
For soup and things served in a bowl.
It's also okay for scooping up peas,
And all foods that tend to roll.

A word about holding your utensil,
The toddler way has to stop.
Hold it almost like a pencil,
Not like a lollipop.

Some foods you can eat with your hands,
Eating them seems like fun.
Burgers, pizza, tacos- use your hands.
Then use your napkin when done.

The size of a bite should be small enough
So you can chew it discreetly.
If a piece of meat is big and tough,
You need to cut it neatly.

Cutting, that's the knife's main task,
It's sharp, so handle with care!
With the fork, hold that meat in place,
Then deftly slice into squares.

Some folks talk with food in their mouth,
I hope that you won't do it!
It's gross and messy and most uncouth,
Just take the time to chew it.

Dinner time is more than just eating,
It's a time to share one's thoughts.
A special time of meeting and greeting,
And having some lively talks.

new teacher

art exhibit

favorite book

friends

soccer game

tasty

butterfly

recess

Reading while dining is seen as rude,
Unless you're dining alone.
Phone use is also poorly viewed,
Your pocket's the place for that phone.

Don't feed the dog or play with your food,
Or slurp or burp or spit.
These actions are all considered crude,
Your grandma will throw a fit!

After eating, don't just get up and leave,
Ask nicely to be excused.
Your request will be well received,
And rarely be refused.

Did I mention "please" and "thank you"?
Those pleasant magical words.
It's amazing what those words can do,
You may get seconds and thirds!

A compliment to the cook or host
Is always appreciated.
The value of a kind word at most
Cannot be overstated.

yummy

delightful   tasty

scrumptious

excellent

delicious

savory

Arf!

You might say "The rolls were so sweet!"
Or else, "The soup tasted fine."
Or, "The flower arrangement was neat,"
Or, "The candles were divine!"

Grandma paused now and took a breath.
"That's a lot to take in.
I hope I haven't bored you to death.
My, what good listeners you've been!"

Lila and Caleb smiled now.
    "We've tried to stay alert.
There is one thing we wondered though,
    Might there be dessert?"

And then they did an awesome thing,
Fulfilling Grandma's wishes.
They began to dance and sing,
And then they washed the dishes!

Table Manners Do's and Don'ts

Do:

Wash your hands before eating

Take off your hat; ask a blessing

Place your napkin on your lap

Pass serving dishes to your left

Hold your utensil like a pencil

Cut large pieces of food into smaller pieces

Engage in pleasant conversation

Use the words "please" and "thank you"

Compliment the cook or host

Ask to be excused before leaving the table

Help with washing the dishes

Don't:

Rest your elbows on the table

Reach in front of someone

Try to eat large pieces of food

Talk with food in your mouth

Read or use your phone at the table

Feed the dog or play with your food

Slurp or burp or spit

ABOUT THE AUTHORS AND ILLUSTRATOR

Robert Wayne and Elizabeth Bode live on a country road in New York's Hudson Valley. They are the proud parents of two and grandparents of six. They were motivated to write *Table Manners* in order to pass on the lessons learned from their parents and grandparents. They previously authored *Gracie and the Real Santa*.

Photo by Liz Crachi

In addition, Robert Wayne Bode is an avid oil painter, often portraying local residents and landscapes. His works have been in several art exhibits, and he previously illustrated *One of Thirteen* and *Gracie and the Real Santa*.

www.ingramcontent.com/pod-product-compliance
Lightning Source LLC
LaVergne TN
LVHW072131070426
835513LV00002B/63

* 9 7 8 1 9 5 5 5 6 8 0 9 8 *